DOES GOD EXIST?

DOES GOD EXIST?
NEW DISCOVERIES

Donald Ackermann

Copyright © 2021 by Donald Ackermann.

All rights reserved. No part of this book may be reproduced in any form or by any electronic or mechanical means, including information storage and retrieval systems, without permission in writing from the publisher, except by reviewers, who may quote brief passages in a review.

ISBN: 978-1-956736-97-7 (Paperback Edition)
ISBN: 978-1-956736-98-4 (Hardcover Edition)
ISBN: 978-1-956736-96-0 (E-book Edition)

Some characters and events in this book are fictitious. Any similarity to the real persons, living or dead, is coincidental and not intended by the author.

Book Ordering Information

Phone Number: 315 288-7939 ext. 1000 or 347-901-4920
Email: info@globalsummithouse.com
Global Summit House
www.globalsummithouse.com

Printed in the United States of America

CONTENTS

PREFACE 1

CAREFUL WHERE YOU STEP 3

EPILOGUE 43

DOES GOD EXIST?
NEW DISCOVERIES
ARE SCIENCE AND THE BELIEF
IN GOD COMPATIBLE? 45

PREFACE

Before we delve into this highly controversial subject, let me say outright that I make no claim to knowing all the answers. While I believe in the existence of a Supreme Being, all I can do is present what we do know to be fact, which will now include many *New Discoveries* made since I first wrote *"Does God Exist?"* But before we go to *"Does God Exist?"*, I want to first tell you a story, a memoir of me at the youthful age of nineteen, soon to be twenty, entitled, *"Careful Where You Step."* You may be scratching your head thinking, what's this got to do with *"Does God Exist?"* Bear with me, and it will become clear.

I was an atheist back then, and you will see in the memoir that because of two men who befriended me, I became enlightened. Had it not been for those two men turning me around, *"Does God Exist?"* may never have been written. So along with the theories and opinions of prominent theologians, scientists, and archeologists— and perhaps a little of my own musings, I leave it to the reader to decide where it takes him or her.

I believe there is such a thing as the soul, and that the soul is intrinsic to man and woman alone, i.e. to human beings. I further believe the vast majority of humanity has, though suppressed, a subconscious, inherent affinity for God. The great physicist, Sir Arthur Eddington, refers to it as ". . . an Inner Light proceeding from a greater power than ours." I have long believed that the pursuit of science itself, at least in part, springs from a desire for answers to questions, which have their roots in our need to know if there is a God. Failure to prove God exists or doesn't exist only causes scientists to intensify their pursuit for answers. For, in spite of their professed disbelief, they too want the answer to be "yes" since only a God can save us from ourselves.

Let me introduce myself. As an author, my writing career spans over fifty years. And since God has granted me a long life, I've seen and experienced an extraordinary number of life events which have given me tremendous insight, enabling me, for instance, to not only write *"Does God Exist?"* but countless essays and commentaries of substance and even the novel, *"The Three Keys"*, the story of a highly principled man fighting to save his marriage and family. In the business of evaluating books, Kirkus Review calls it *"a tale of morality and honesty."* Foreword Clarion Review states, *"Ackermann's storytelling is methodical and precise, driven by action rather than emotion."* And BlueInk Review says *"will resonate with anyone who has ever tried to be a stand-up guy or gal in a complicated world."*

I tell you, the reader, this to demonstrate that no one could have written a novel of such substance and depth without having lived a genuinely compelling life himself. That same principle applies to having written: *"Does God Exist?"* I've known what it is to have been an atheist when I was younger and working as a land surveyor in Louisiana with two God-fearing black men who convinced me that God does exist. And I've known what it is, subsequently, to fervently believe in God after having lived that part of the extraordinary life I spoke of before. So come, journey with me into the mysterious, the uncertain, the unknown, and let's see where it takes us.

CAREFUL WHERE YOU STEP

We were three restless young men, tired of having nothing to do but hang around the street, drink when we could get it, and chase the girls. We were ready for an adventure, something different, something exciting. Blame it on spring fever; it was early March, 1950.

At eighteen, Harry was the youngest and the most laid back. Wavy black hair and slim to the point of being skinny, he could be easily led. Al, twenty, and just the opposite, he was a user and could be aggressive. At five feet, ten inches with thin blond hair, he was the biggest and not afraid to throw his weight around. I don't know why I hung around with him. Not really my kind of friend. We clashed at times.

As for me, Don, I was considered the serious, sensitive guy in the gang and looked to for an honest and fair answer when a dispute arose. We were members of a much bigger neighborhood gang that had grown up together in roach-infested tenements in the heart of Plainfield, New Jersey. My parents lost our house during the Great Depression back in 1931. The only one with a steady job as a rodman with a land surveying firm made me the only one of the three of us with any money. But I wasn't rich, giving half to my mom who always had to run around the corner to Personal Finance every month for a temporary loan to make ends meet due to my drunken father, whom I didn't get along with, drinking up his wages. Close to turning twenty and though only five feet, eight inches, I was wiry and could handle myself in a fight. In our neighborhood, you'd better be able to fight. But I never told my father I could fight. I let him continue to stew, thinking I wasn't that rough, tough son he wanted. And maybe I wasn't. But I just let him stew, believing that it is a form of revenge for his holding me at arms-length.

Much to the dismay of my parents, I announced I quit my job and heading for Louisiana with two of the guys, using as an excuse that two of our buddies, Frank and Jim who had enlisted in the Army Airforce, were stationed in Shreveport. But I knew we would first go to New Orleans and live it up. That part I didn't mention.

A couple of days later, we all piled into my cramped, beat-up, 1941 Plymouth Coupe freshly painted maroon. The car wasn't made for a back seat, but somehow I squeezed one in that I had picked up at the local junkyard. The seat insisted on tilting forward, so I propped the front of the seat up with woodblocks. They had turned black from all the drinking (and vomiting) that went on in the car. Yeah, we were wild and bad—or so we thought.

I did the driving. With no superhighways back then, it would mean traveling just local highways and roads. I had laid out the route I would take on a map of the Eastern United States and a written list of roads and turns to be made. Not straight as the crow flies, it would be more than thirteen hundred miles. And, feeling "invincible," I was determined to drive every bit of it myself . . . nonstop. Or was it because I didn't trust my buddies behind the wheel of my pride and joy? Al had badly damaged the car before when I loaned it to him for a date.

All went well until I hit the many twists and turns through the Blue Ridge Mountains of Tennessee, which put me on edge. I was relieved to hit Arkansas but not for long. We went from twists and turns to potholes big enough and deep enough to do some real damage. At this point, I had to fight dozing off, but the jolts served the purpose of helping me stay awake. Little did my friends, both sleeping most of the time, know how close they came to a head-on collision more than once. But I was invincible . . . onward.

We entered northern Louisiana, and the roads got smoother. I noticed a rhythmic thump, thump, thump coming from one of the tires. As I drove, it became more pronounced. I pulled over onto the gravel shoulder to take a look. My buddies finally woke up thinking we were in New Orleans already but, eying the rural desolation, soon realized we weren't and joined me.

It didn't take long to find out what the thumping was all about. A big bubble on the front right tire bulged out over an inch from the main tread. Closer examination proved it to be a patch job with no rubber left on the patch itself. I could see the rayon lining ready to blow. That's what we were riding on. The whole tire, for that matter, was a retread, a tire that had gone bald and then had new groves cut into the bald rubber to make it look newer. Just wait until I get home and confront the guy who sold it to me.

We went to put the spare on but found it flat. We'd have to take our chances driving and stop at the first gas station we came to and inflate the spare so we could get the thumper off. Mission accomplished, but we now had to drive without a spare.

We resumed our trip and arrived in New Orleans the afternoon of our second day on the road. Our first priority had to be to find a room we could afford, or in truth that I could afford, Al and Harry having very little money. Not easy. We decided on a small room with one bureau, a well-worn stuffed chair, and one single and one double bed. Even though a bit seedy, the dated hotel served our purpose, and we settled in. Beggars can't be choosy.

That evening, we roamed about trying to get a feel for the city. Around six o'clock, we were treated to this tremendous cloudburst, violent thunder, and lightning. Canal Street, the main drag and very wide, soon became a river going downhill. We couldn't believe it as we stood there soaked, but the locals, seemingly used to this and oblivious to the flooding, just continued going about their business, holding umbrellas or newspapers up. The torrential downpour ended as abruptly as it had started. Half an hour later, Canal Street showed only some lingering puddles.

We continued to wander as night descended, finding some of the street lamps quaint compared to those back home. Hungry, the three of us decided to try a Po boy, essentially a potato sandwich, Po an abbreviation for poor, i.e., a poor boy's sandwich. Surprisingly delicious and very satisfying, we now looked for a lively night spot and some serious drinking. We found it on Bourbon Street and its storied Red Light district in the French Quarter. The Red Light District, with its neon lights and many overhanging balconies, got its nickname, Storyville, because party time reigned supreme continuously, it being the only part of New Orleans where legalized prostitution flourished.

Who said southern gals didn't like Yankees? We couldn't get away from them. Maybe they thought we had a lot of money. Ha! if they only knew. We did a lot of dancing, the gals not hesitating to rub their bodies up against yours or tongue your ear. Getting laid was for the asking but, in our own private little assessment, we all agreed that catching something from this bunch was a little too risky . . . and likely. So, in spite of our semi erections, we split.

We resumed roaming the narrow and ill-lit streets. Many entrances to buildings were recessed and dark, conducive for a woman or female teenager to lurk in the shadows. As we passed one of these recessed doorways, a woman grabbed me by the arm and pulled me to her.

"Five dollars," she murmured between puffs on a cigarette.

"No, thanks," I said and pulled away.

"Go ahead," coaxed Al. "We'll wait."

"You'll wait, huh. I'll tell you what, Al, if you're so gung ho about her, why don't Harry and I wait for you."

"Are you kidding," Al replied.

"I see. It's okay for you to try to push me into doing something you yourself wouldn't do. That's just like you, Al. Just like you."

At three in the morning, we fell into our beds, half-drunk and exhausted. Al got up first that morning, already eleven o'clock. If he couldn't sleep, neither would we. He kicked our bed. The first order of business had to be breakfast. We knew of a small restaurant around the corner, and that's where we headed. The boss, a rather plump man who perhaps ate too much of his own cooking, had a heavy beard. He seemed to have a bit of a French dialect, as did many locals, some referred to as Canuks, suggesting French Canadian descent.

After packing away the pancakes, we hit the streets. The city hummed with social life. We took to roaming again, taking in the sights. Now daytime, much more of the city came to light. Substantial traffic cruised Canal Street, including buses electrified by overhead wires or an occasional electrified trolley that still ran on tracks implanted in Canal Street. People hustled from store to store, displaying a lot of wares different from back home, especially clothes. But inevitably, the southern gals drew all our attention. Standing on a busy corner, we gave them the eye. I didn't know about Al or Harry, but things were starting to stir below my belt.

"Enough," I said. "Let's go to The Get Together Club where we were last night. I like that place, a lot of action."

"I'm with you," said Harry.

Not being all that familiar with the city, we experienced some difficulty trying to retrace the previous night's steps, but determination won out. Like all young people there, we did a lot of dancing and drinking. Al threw caution to the wind and got laid in some back room where "things" went on. We packed it in around two and crashed in our room drunk and played out.

After four days of this debauchery, we had what would prove to be a game-changing argument. What little money Al and Harry had quickly evaporated. I footed the bill for eating, drinking, the weekly rent, everything. With little money left, I suggested we all had to find jobs, even part time jobs would be better than nothing. Al exploded.

"Fuck you! if you think I'm going to go to work. I came down here to have some fun."

"Yeah, well, so did I, Al, but what on?" I yelled back. "It takes money to live and have fun, and I'm damn near tapped out."

"So you go to fuck to work," Al said, pointing a finger at me.

"You've got some nerve, Al. As if I had to twist your arm. You raved about coming to New Orleans first before going on to Shreveport to pick up Frank and take him home."

"What's happening here?" asked Harry. "We're supposed to be friends, right? Let's calm down and figure this out."

"You figure it out, Harry," said Al. "I know what I'm going to do."

"Yeah? How?" I said. "I should have known how you'd be. You never went to work back home after your short stint in the Army and, by the way, never told us why they discharged you so soon either."

"I think Don is right, Al," said Harry. "We all have to come up with some money if we're going to make it."

"Fuck you too, Harry," yelled Al. "I knew you'd side with him."

"Well, what's right is right," replied Harry.

"I said fuck you too, Harry."

"Since you don't give a shit about being fair, Al, here's my solution," I said, pointedly directing what I had to say at him, not Harry. "From now on I'm only paying for what I order at the dinner, not what you order, Al. And when you can't pay, maybe they'll let you wash dishes."

I saw it coming. The words no sooner left my mouth than Al swung at me. I succeeded in deflecting the blow, but the jolt sent a cascade of my usually well-groomed brown hair over my eyes. He was bigger and probably stronger, but I didn't fear him and could fight. We struggled, fists meeting their mark. Over one bed we tumbled and rolled onto the floor before coming up swinging again. Normally shy Harry dove headlong, forcing himself between us.

"Come on you guys, break it up," he shouted. "Want to get us kicked out?"

With Harry in the way, we both held our punches. Some semblance of order returned, but we all knew then and there things would never be the same. It had been coming for a long time between Al and me. Harry decided to call it quits and used a hotel phone to call home. His mother wired money to the local Western Union for airfare. He took a taxi to the airport.

Al said he wanted to get drunk and had the gall to ask if I would give him a five. I deliberately did just to get rid of him. By the time he got back, I too intended to be gone. I had known Al to be a bastard back home, but I never realized just how selfish and much of a bastard he could be. Not really my kind of guy, how could we have ever been friends?

With Al gone, I hastily scoured the want ads in the local newspaper in the hotel lobby for a job—any job. It jumped out at me; a land surveyor looking for a man who knew how to run a transit, an instrument calibrated for laying out angles and distances. I knew how to do that.

. . .

As rodman, low man in a three-man survey field crew back home, I learned fast how to operate a transit so I could move up to transit man and make more money. I even studied a survey book to learn the nuts and bolts of how to actually survey a piece of land, my goal being to advance to party chief who heads the three-man crew. But you had to have a lot of experience and know a lot to make party chief. Ultimately, the goal would be to qualify for taking the state exam and get my license as a professional land surveyor. I could then command much more money or even open my own business. This is the kind of dream I walked away from just to give my buddy a ride back home, a stupid decision by a foolish young man.

I found a public phone booth and called the surveyor. A guy

named John picked up and informed me he was staying right here in New Orleans while looking for a transit man. I agreed to meet him in his hotel room. A knock on the door brought a red-headed, freckled face, disheveled man of about fifty. He invited me in, and we sat down in a small living room. He had an accent that seemed to me a cross between a Texan and a southerner.

Naturally, he wanted a rundown on my experience. I knew he could see I was young, so I started doing a dance hoping to dispel the possibility my youth might be a negative in his mind. I normally never lied outright about anything but, if I wanted the job, and I really did need the job, I might have to exaggerate a little here and there.

I told him I had been working with a field crew for a year; exaggeration number one for it had only been nine months. I told him I ran the transit back home; exaggeration number two for, though pretty good at it already, I was only a rodman and still learning. He seemed to buy it but saved a test question for last.

"How much does one minute of arc make one hundred feet away?"

He could have asked dozens of questions I would not have been able to answer but, thank God, I had studied the survey book at times. "Three-hundredths of a foot," I answered.

"Good man! You're hired."

Quite proud of myself for having held my own, he then dropped a bomb on me.

"I've been hired to lay out the planned route for a new Texaco pipeline through the swamps, you know, bayou country. You're familiar with the bayou down here, aren't you?"

"I've read about it."

"You'll be in charge of a seven-man crew that will drive stakes marking the route and clear the way using machetes and brush hooks. You've probably used them back home."

"I've used both, machetes a lot," I said.

John continued. "You will actually lay out the pipeline's route, which is mainly straight but has a few angles."

I began to feel queasy in the stomach. I thought I'd be running the gun directly under him. The ad said nothing about taking charge of laying out the route for a new Texaco pipeline. That smacked heavy duty for an about-to-turn-twenty nineteen-year-old with a lousy nine months experience under his belt. I didn't know what to do. Should I be more truthful with John and turn the job down? I didn't want to screw up the route and cause him serious trouble.

He saw me shaken. "What's the matter? Afraid you can't handle it? Speak up now, Don, I don't want to waste my time."

"I'm not sure," I said. "I' m not sure I know enough."

"Can you run the transit?"

"Yes, but---"

"Then you'll be alright. I'll be coming out once in a while to see how you're doing. And I'll be shooting Polaris every night to make sure you're staying on route."

"Well, that makes me feel a little better, John."

"Good. Then it's settled. The pay will be three bucks an hour, which I know is probably triple of what you were making back home. But then there aren't too many guys willing to work in the bayou. Is that satisfactory?"

"Holy mackerel, I'll be rich! Yes, sir!"

"Be here seven Monday morning and follow me to my place where you can leave your car. We'll use my station wagon and find a place to stay not too far from where we'll be working. I know a good boarding house in the area."

I made it to the Roadside Motel, where John stayed at quarter to seven. There were three motley-looking characters hanging around, apparently waiting for John to come out. They were unshaven, dirty, dressed in filthy clothes that looked like they hadn't seen a washing machine for months. They were talking haltingly amongst themselves and, from what little I could hear, not sounding all that well educated. They eyed me warily. *Good God*, I thought to myself. *Are these the guys I'm supposed to work with? I hope not.*

Suddenly, a motel room door flung open with John heading straight for his station wagon all business. He hadn't closed the motel door behind him, and one could see well into the room, including the bed. It looked in shambles, as if he had had a terrible wrestling match with the bedding, perhaps a fitful tormenting sleep.

"All right, what are you guys waiting for? Get in," he ordered.

The wagon was a big eight-seater. I headed for the back seat but, hearing John chastise me, stopped abruptly.

"What the fuck are you doing? *They* sit in the back seat not you. In my absence you're the boss, and don't you forget it. So if you're going to *be* the boss, *act* like the boss. Get your ass the hell up here with me"

"Sorry." I knew he was right, but it bothers me when he is treating the men like they were something less than human. Don't ask me where I got it from, but I had always believed everyone should be treated equally and with respect, no matter how low on the totem pole they were.

"And don't apologize. You're young but you'll get there."

John came on strong, showing his true self now: direct and no-nonsense. He had things to get done and intended to get them done. Gone was the more polished surveyor he had presented during the interview.

We drove for about ten minutes when we came to a construction site. A building was being built, and some ditch digging had been going on for gas, water, and sewer connections. The three men got out. Evidently, this is what they had been doing and why they were so dirty. It made me wonder just how many jobs John had going.

John next drove me to the boarding house where I would be staying but only to show me its location before going on to the job, the proposed Texaco pipeline.

"I'll introduce you to your crew and get you started and then I'm leaving. I never asked, but I hope you don't mind working with niggers."

"You mean Negroes?"

"Is that what they call them up north?"

"That's what *I* call them. And yes, I can work with them. I can work with anybody." I had to fight the urge to do battle, job or no job, but thought better of it. John probably sensed as much from the tone of my answer; an uncomfortable silence settled in during the rest of the trip.

He pulled up to a group of men, some standing some squatting. One man stood out immediately, Jim, a big burly black man with powerful looking muscular arms, a tinge of gray creeping into his black hair. He would be the crew leader John told me and back up my orders if necessary. A second black man, Mike, stood almost as big as Jim. I got the impression from how they kind of spoke as one that they were buddies.

Old Joe, who seemed to have kind of a French accent, was a short, thin, wiry man, perhaps fifty-five and still sporting a full head of hair. He warmed up to me. Having worked in the bayou many times, he tried to tell me, when he could get a word in edgewise, some history about the bayou and how to handle myself. A lively animated man, he seemed quite happy with the life he had carved out for himself.

Also having a French accent, Pierre looked to be about thirty and came across as being very confident. He regularly hunted alligators for their skin, for which a big market existed for making pocketbooks, shoes, belts, and the like. He warned me that when walking the bayou, I would have to be very careful to learn how. The first couple of times, he would be glad to show me what he meant. I would have to step where he stepped on what he called floats, a solid mass of intertwined vegetative growth. "Careful where you step and learn to recognize which ones will support a man as opposed to those on which you would go right down in the swamp water."

Eduardo, a second-generation Mexican, Austin, named after the capitol of Texas, and Luke from Arkansas rounded out the seven-man crew I'd be working with. Relatively new to the job, they had been working with Jim and the others only for the past two weeks. They laid back and had little to say.

With introductions over, I mounted the transit on its tripod and followed John. Hidden by a small patch of woods, I had no idea how close the swamp lay. Pierre took charge, shouldering the transit while I navigated a stretch of swamp. John followed behind.

"Now, careful where you step. Only step exactly where I step or you're going down. You're not going to drown, the water's not deep. But I'll tell you now, those ankle boots won't do. They're going to get filled with water and water ants."

"Water ants!"

"Yes, water ants. And they bite. With those boots you'd end up having to work the whole day out here with them biting. And don't forget, sometimes there's a nice, hungry, quiet gator down there waiting for his next meal."

Damn, I thought to myself. *John didn't say anything about this shit when he interviewed me. Hell, why would he? He knew I'd probably walk. Fuck me. What have I gotten myself into?*

"Ready, boss?" I heard Pierre ask, snapping me out of my mental assessment of being trapped in what looked more and more like a shitty predicament.

"Yeah, I'm ready, Pierre."

"Now remember, my foot will leave a slight footprint on the float. That's where you'll put your foot. And whatever foot I use you use so they'll match. If you pay attention, you'll be surprised how fast you'll learn to tell a safe float and one that's not safe. Here we go."

With those words of wisdom, Pierre took his first step. The float, about four feet in diameter, hardly gave an inch. Even though he had a longer stride, I managed to follow him, nervous but successfully. And he was right. I already started to see the difference between the floats he favored and the ones he avoided, where the vegetation looked a little loose and appeared to have just a little water lying on the top.

We made it to an area where the floats disappeared, just shallow swamp water. The crew had gathered where they had left off the previous week. John showed me the last cedar stake set, and I set up the transit centered over it. Looking back up the line that had been trimmed clear, I could see in the distance a fine cross marked on a wood lath set about six hundred feet away. I locked the transit's crosshairs on it and flipped the transit's scope over so as to look the other way where we would continue clearing and staking the route. Feeling intimidated being the boss over all these older and more mature men, I struggled to find myself. John's words came back to me: *If you're going to be the boss, act like the boss.*

Stay calm, assert yourself, Don, speak with authority. "Okay guys, start trimming. Joe, you walk down five or six hundred feet away and set a lath for the men to trim to. I'll keep you on line and give you line for setting the lath." *Stay with it, Don, stay with it.*

I picked old Joe for that job because everyone said he had the eyes of an eagle despite his age. He did what I told him to do, the men started chopping, and we were on our way. *Son of a gun, maybe I can run the job. Don't get cocky, Don. It's only the beginning.*

"I know you were afraid you couldn't handle the job," said John, "but I knew you could. Otherwise I wouldn't have hired you. You're a smart kid, Don, I can tell. So don't sell yourself short. You just got to get over the jitters."

"I think I'm already starting to feel a little better, John."

"There you go. Just keep the men moving and remember

you're the boss. They'll listen to you because they can already see you know what you're doing. This line is over three miles long so, like I said, keep the men moving. Right now, we're on target to meet my contract deadline with Texaco, and I want to keep it that way."

"Yes-sir."

"I won't be back today. The men will show you a better way out. You won't have to worry about stepping on floats. Pierre just tried to teach you how because sometimes we run into them. Any questions?"

"Where do we meet every morning?"

"At Pierre's house, it's on stilts. He's lived in the bayou all his life, Makes his living off the swamp. Helps us out now and then. Anything else?"

"No. I think that's it, John."

"Good. I'm out of here."

John walked back up the previously trimmed line and disappeared. Now I was really in charge . . . and on my own.

. . .

The boarding house looked immense. It had to be if it were to accommodate so many men who couldn't find work at home or maybe just preferred living on the road. They came from all over: Texas, Arkansas, Missouri, Mississippi and, of course, Louisiana itself.

The sprawling grounds included a big farming area where the owners grew most of the food they served. Several huge garages housed the cars, trucks, and farming equipment. The substantial home where the owners lived included a spacious dining hall for the lodgers.

I had to share my room with another guy. We each had our own bunk bed with plenty of space underneath for storing personal stuff. The shower room, centrally located, serviced four surrounding rooms, which meant for the eight guys living in them. It didn't bother me showering naked amongst a bunch of other naked guys. We were all hung the same way, more or less.

Chow time ran between the hours of six and eight for breakfast and supper. You either made it then, or you didn't eat. The table in the dining hall had to be at least twenty-five feet long with, it looked to me, about a couple dozen men noisily trying to talk while still cramming the beef stew and bread down. I saw an opening next to my roommate and sat down, hoping to get acquainted. From Texas, his name was Travis, he was twenty-two, and with me just turning twenty, I figured we could relate and really hit it off.

With his father having lost a leg in an oil rig accident, Travis took on being the family breadwinner. He had been making a little money with brief part time jobs back home, but now he had to make some serious money. With no decent jobs where he lived in Texas, he came to Louisiana, which boasted a lot of work for the asking.

"Yeah, I'm glad I came here. I've been pulling down about a hundred-fifty a week, a hundred of which I send home to Mom."

Travis said that with some pride in his voice as he ran his fingers through a healthy crop of wavy brown hair. He looked to be six feet tall, slim, and obviously in good shape. But what really struck me, given what had happened to his father, was that he stepped up to the plate and took care of his family, my kind of guy.

"How 'bout you, Don, you Yankee fuck?" We both laughed. "Why are you down here?"

Oh, I quit my job back home, which may have been a big mistake, and came down here to take my buddy who's stationed at the Army Air Force base in Shreveport home when he goes on furlough for a couple of weeks in May."

"So what are you doing for money?"

"I lucked out and got this job helping to survey the route for a proposed Texaco pipeline through the bayou. That's the kind of job I had back home, land surveying. How about you?"

"I drive a truck for a lumber company. Right now I'm delivering lumber every day to this housing development." Travis seemed to ponder something.

"Surveying, huh. You look a little brainy." We chuckled. "Hey, enough of this shit. What do you say we go into town, what there is of it. There's a tavern and a couple of gals I'm in pretty good with. I know I could get laid, Sarah, if I had a buddy to take care of her girlfriend, Jean. They're both decent-looking chicks, and Jean has big ones," Travis said, cupping both hands to his chest. "Hey, if one fucks they both fuck. I know I could get you laid too. Unless, of course, that isn't your bag."

"What are you, crazy? After you get me all worked up with the prospects." I pulled on my crotch to make a little more room.

"I figured you might be horny. So-o, what do you say? Let's go"

We drove into town, not much more than a hamlet, in his '46 Chevy. I saw the tavern he spoke of. It sounded lively; I could hear music, chatter, and laughter. We went in, looked around, and made a beeline for the only remaining empty bar stools at the end of the bar. We settled in with a couple of bottles of Dickson's Beer, which I never heard of. The nightspot, decent and bigger than it looked to be from the outside, had a lot of wall paneling and woodwork. The tavern obviously had some history, pictures of a lot of locals down through the years plastered on the back wall above the many bottles of booze.

We'd been there a half hour and Travis began apologizing for the girls not being there when in they walked. They spotted Travis and came right over to us. One drew close to him, presumably Sarah. She had a stunning figure. He put an arm around her waist.

"Sarah, Jean, this is my buddy, Don. Don, this is Jean." She was kind of pretty with strawberry blond hair and, though we had just met, she cozied up to me.

"Going to buy me a drink?"

"Absolutely, what's you're thing?"

"Same as you're drinking."

"I was beginning to think you didn't have any buddies, Travis," said Sarah, pushing back her long black hair. "Now we all can have some fun."

We did a lot of dancing, drinking, and light kissing. But the heat coursing through our veins couldn't be contained any longer. The girls took us to an old, small, one-bedroom house they rented. From there, it was all sex. We stripped with total disregard for any modesty. Travis climbed with Sarah into her bed, and Jean and I climbed into hers. They assured us they couldn't get pregnant. I was so starved we didn't waste any time and got with it. Finally, from sheer exhaustion we fell asleep.

We made a weekend of it and didn't really want to leave Sunday either, but we split around two in the morning, not wanting to lose our jobs. This didn't leave much time for sleep but, we were young, who cared.

I went directly to the job Monday morning, my crew already waiting for me there. Soon the first week passed and we were now operating like a well-oiled machine. I had lost my jitters. Almost a full mile of the proposed route had been trimmed, staked, and established. All went well. I treated the men with respect and, in turn, they respected me and worked hard.

Then, in the middle of the second week, I forgot to brown bag it. Well, these guys weren't about to let me go hungry, no way. As we gathered for lunch sitting where we could, an old rotting trunk of a swamp maple that had once flourished or on a bit of high ground, Jim and Mike offered me some of their sandwiches. Reluctant to eat up their food, I waved them off. "Hey, it's me who forgot his lunch, Jim. I deserve to go hungry."

"That's not what God says."

Whoa, where did that come from? I thought. From previous talk I had gotten the impression the two Negroes were religious; I just didn't know how much. I didn't want to offend them, whether about God or not wanting their sandwiches because they were black, so I ate their sandwiches and drank their coffee, awfully strong and laced with chicory.

Things got uncomfortably quiet while we ate. I caught Jim and Mike staring at me most of the time and sensed something coming. I wasn't wrong.

"You, Yankee," said Mike, "you believe in God?"

That question caught me completely off guard. He had touched upon a sore spot with me. While brought up Catholic and making my First Communion and Confirmation, I had lost faith because of a couple of incidents involving our priests. Being honest and sincere, I had confessed when twelve to masturbating. Not a good thing to do with what that led to. The priest warned me if I kept doing that, my brain would turn to water. That night in my sleep, whenever I moved my head, I thought I heard water sloshing around. Scared to death, I got up the courage to ask our family doctor and, of course, he said the priest never should have told me that because it's not true. The other incident involved a different priest propositioning my mom. When I overheard her tell my father that, I made up my mind and broke with the church, and ever since, I had been carrying on a running feud with God.

"You haven't answered me," said Mike, snapping me back to the present. The other guys had taken note of the exchange and waited in silence to see where things went.

"Look, Mike, I'm Catholic; doesn't that answer your question?"

"No," said Jim. "Do you believe in God?"

I continued trying to do a dance. "He's supposed to be everywhere."

"Not supposed to be, he *is* everywhere," declared Mike.

"So do you believe in God?" demanded Jim once more.

I could see they were not going to let me go. Not wanting to cause them to get even more antagonistic, I gave them what they wanted. "Yeah, I guess so."

"You *guess* so?" said Mike, no longer trying to hide the anger rising in him.

No use, they had me backed into a corner. "Yeah, yeah, I do believe in God."

"That's better," said Jim. "Otherwise, you might not walk out of here."

That totally unexpected threat from guys I had been getting along with so well didn't set well with me. That is, if they really meant it, and at the moment I didn't believe they did. But I had to probe a little. "I thought we were friends."

"We are again now," said Jim. He stuck out his hand, we shook. Then Mike and I shook.

"I'm glad because I really like you guys," I said.

The other men relaxed, seeing the clash subside. We went about our business and got another eight hundred feet trimmed and staked that afternoon.

Our relationship seemingly returned to what it had been. The fact that it happened made me feel a little uncomfortable again and start wondering. *Did these guys really respect this Yankee, or were they just following my orders because they didn't want to lose their jobs?*

Friday night and payday, Travis sat on his bunk, writing a letter to his mom. He would take his chances and double-wrap eighty dollars in writing paper and mail it with the letter like he had been doing. Getting this done took priority with him, so we saved going into town for Saturday and hit the sack early.

I was jolted out of a deep sleep by the violent shaking of the whole building. A terrible deafening roar of wind engulfed me, like that of a speeding freight train that had me pinned to the tracks while racing right over me..

"What the hell's going on?" I yelled to Travis, who had hopped out of his bunk.

"Lay on the floor under your bunk as much as possible!" he screamed. "It's a tornado!"

"Holy shit!, a tornado!" I yelled, scrambling to the floor and jamming myself halfway under my bunk.

"Stay there, man, this fucker's a bad one . . . and close."

We both froze. It took a good five minutes before we could hear the sound of the wind starting to diminish and the twister slowly moving away.

"Fuck me, Travis," I said, as we both crawled out from under our bunks and stood up.

Travis laughed. "Hey, get used to it. We have them down here. I just don't like it when they get that close. Back home we have an in-ground cellar to retreat to, a lot safer."

"You have them in Texas too?"

"Sure do, a lot more than Louisiana."

"And I'm headed for Texas next week. That's just great."

We climbed back into our bunks. Travis snored in no time but not me. I lay there wide-eyed, my mind going a mile a minute. But eventually, I did fall asleep and woke to a bright sunny morning. I looked out the window. The old barn had been torn apart, its wood planking scattered all over the place along with all kinds of things: lawn chairs, tables, bottles, clothing, you name it. I craned my neck to get a look at the main house and dining hall. It still stood. Thank God.

I found it hard to believe but our host still served a breakfast of scrambled eggs, bacon, potatoes, toast and coffee right on time as if nothing had happened. The locals rushed around most of them carrying fishing poles and bait. Travis filled me in. Saturday morning was fishing time and nothing, not even a tornado, would put a damper on tradition. Sure enough soon the place looked deserted; the wreckage could just lay right there. "They'll get to it when they feel like it," he said. I couldn't help but admire the resilience, the spirit of these Louisianans.

That same Saturday over a few beers I talked to Travis about the threat from Jim and Mike. I wanted to make sure I had my head on straight in thinking they really didn't mean it. Early in the evening, the tavern relatively quiet, I needed to get someone else's opinion.

"I don't think they would have done anything even if you told them you didn't believe in God," Travis said.

"You don't think so, huh? Well, they sure seemed serious."

"Look, Don, you have to understand. Blacks down here are much more religious than whites. You being a Yankee didn't help. Haven't you ever heard a black congregation singing those Gospel songs in church? They really get emotional, and all worked up because they really do believe in God. They feel their belief in God, and it shows when they sing."

"I guess you're right, Travis. Even up north, they appear to be more religious than us whites. I wonder why that is?"

The girls never showed despite it being Saturday night. Frustrated, we got pretty drunk before heading for the boarding house and crapping out. But come Sunday evening, we were right back in the tavern drinking again. This time things were different.

"Look who just walked in," Travis said, giving me the elbow.

I didn't have to look because Sarah and Jean came right over to us. It didn't take long for the four of us to be in heat again and, after a couple of hours of drinking and rubbing bodies, we headed for Sarah and Jean's place. The evening proved to be a repeat performance, but we left by midnight having to be out on our jobs early.

The next day brought more trudging through the swamps. With the persistent water ants and other strange water creatures driving me crazy, I had bought knee boots to keep them out. But in place of them, big striped ferocious mosquitos relentlessly attacked us and the water moccasins became more plentiful. Extremely poisonous, I chose to be wary of them and struck out at them with my machete if they got too close.

I saw only two alligators in all this time, but I knew plenty more lived here in the bayou. I could hear the gurgling of gas in their stomachs as they lay in their underwater nests. And then it happened while giving old Joe far away line. I heard some splashing-like noise behind me. I turned and saw the biggest gator I had ever seen coming for me. I moved to the other side of the transit, hoping to keep it between us. Stupid me if I thought for one minute that gator couldn't just thrust himself through the tripod legs and get me. But I didn't know what else to do.

"Jim! Mike! Somebody! Help!"

Apparently, gators aren't too smart because even though

he could have lunged right through the tripod legs, he chose to go around them. And so did I, determined to keep the tripod between us.

"Jim! Mike! Help! Help!"

The alligator, frustrated, finally decided to push right through the tripod. I got ready to run, but in their natural element, alligators are a lot faster than people think. I thought to myself, *well, maybe this is it.*

Just as the gator made his move, I saw a big double-edged ax high in the air. In my fear, I never even saw Jim come running. With powerful arms, he brought the ax down hard on the alligator's back, slicing through its spine. The gator lay there paralyzed.

Inclined to fall all over Jim with gratitude, he waved me off and instead wrapped his arms around me and gave me a big hug. "You okay?"

"Yeah, I'm okay, Jim, Thanks." *And this is the guy who supposedly threatened me? I should have known that anyone who believes in God as genuinely as Jim does could never do another human being harm.*

We pushed hard for the next couple of weeks and finished laying out this three-mile segment of the proposed Texaco pipeline. On our final day in the bayou, I decided to keep count of how many water moccasins I saw. Incredibly, the tally ran to fifty-one and, wouldn't you know it, the very last one was gigantic and attacked me. While walking on high ground, deliberately created from dredging piled so as to avoid having to walk in the swamp water, she attacked. I assumed the snake to be a mother, probably defending a nest full of young. She came up out of the water and launched her attack, mouth wide open—and what a mouth. I struck at her with my machete while backing away. She moved faster than I thought any snake could move. I repeatedly missed the only target I had, her mouth. Finally, I connected and really hurt her, her mouth bleeding profusely. She retreated and slithered back down into the water. I found myself hoping she'd live for the sake of her young. After all, this was *her* home, *I* was the invader.

With our work done in Louisiana, John held a meeting to brief us on where we were headed next. It would be Texas. "I think you'll like it a lot better there, no swamps, just dry land. We'll be laying out another segment for the pipeline in east Texas. The one thing you'll have to put up with is heat. Oh, yes, you'll also have to watch out for the red bulls, especially if there are cows around he considers his."

"Great," I said. "We go from alligators and water moccasins to red bulls." Everyone laughed.

We paid one last visit to the girls, of course. Travis and I had become such good friends we found parting depressing. Not wanting to lose touch, we exchanged home addresses and phone numbers. With that, we shook hands, and I went off to Texas.

. . .

We left around six in the morning. It would be a seven-hour trip to Center City, Texas, all over back roads and some main country roads but no highways until we hit Texas, me following John in my aging Plymouth. Bugs thrive in Louisiana's semi-tropical climate. They squashed by the hundreds making a real mess of my grill and windshield before we got into Texas. We pulled up to an old hotel that had obviously seen better days but would serve as our home for a while.

There was nobody to be seen, the town seemingly deserted. Though only late April, the sun, directly overhead, beat down on us unmercifully. Well, John warned us it would be hot. But he didn't say anything about it being a dustbowl, little dirt devils swirling about here and there, making breathing precarious and irritating our eyes. We unloaded, got our rooms, and by five o'clock, settled in.

To keep costs down, we doubled up in small rooms furnished with two single beds. I had the privilege of rooming with John again. He seemed to have this thing about bosses sticking together and not fraternizing with those who did the dog work; a little bit like in military service where officers are discouraged from fraternizing with the enlisted men and women.

We found the small hotel restaurant nothing like the immense and informal boarding house dining room. Once more, John maneuvered us to our own table, which I found a bit disturbing. I had taken a liking to mixing with the guys, especially Jim, Mike, and old Joe. John seemed like such an ordinary, down-to-earth guy who could mix with anybody; I couldn't understand why he behaved this way with the crew.

I awoke several times during the night due to John's violent tossing and turning. He constantly argued with someone in his dream—unquestionably more like a nightmare. From what little I could catch, it sounded like he was having it out with some woman, accusing her of cheating on him. I found it difficult to get a good night's sleep with him erupting every so often.

The first to awaken at daybreak, I saw John hanging naked half in half out of bed all twisted up in the sheet and blanket jumbled something awful, as if he had had a life and death wrestling match with his antagonist. When he awoke, I didn't know what to say. Embarrassed, he apologized profusely if he had kept me awake. This became a nightly event.

Things started to become a little clearer to me now. I felt I had him figured out. He didn't want to get too chummy or room with any of the other guys because he didn't want them to know he had psychological problems. He had to appear strong and in control. But how about me? The only thing I could think of is that he apparently trusted me to be more understanding for some reason and say nothing. And I didn't. I never even asked him about his problem or if I could help. I think he appreciated that.

Early that morning, we made it to the job, a big ranch and pasture where Texaco had bought rights to a pipeline easement fifty feet wide. We met the owner, a man in his seventies with unruly graying hair and a robust outdoor complexion. He told us emphatically that no tree with a trunk over eight inches in diameter should be cut down under no circumstances. I set his mind at ease by telling him we could triangulate around a tree without trying to explain to him what triangulation meant. I understood his passion for trees. I too had an inherent love for big majestic trees like the American Elm, American Beech, and especially the Giant Sequoia Redwoods out in California.

We could really move on dry ground as opposed to sloshing around in the swamp and laid out three thousand feet of the route. With a long trudge back to the trucks, I decided to call it quits late afternoon. Soaked with sweat like the rest of the crew, I desperately needed a shower and to cool down.

After chow, we wandered around Center City, which took all of about fifteen minutes, the town being so small. A few stores: hardware, spirits, a small grocery, and a one-pump gas station closed half the time rounded out the so-called business district. But where were the natives? Who knew? With nowhere to go and nothing to do, we hit the one place always open: the liquor store.

The booze flowed freely, mainly beer but some hard stuff too.

We sat around on the hotel porch feeling pretty good when John showed up. He stopped long enough to chat a little and have a quick shot of whiskey then left for our room. By twelve o'clock we figured we'd better do the same.

The next morning we picked up where we left off, punching this stretch of the proposed pipeline southeast toward Louisiana for a hookup with the route through the bayou country we had just left. No water ants here, but there were mosquitos, and those vicious horse flies preying upon the horses and cattle . . . and now us. While our host did keep a few sheep, this was essentially cattle country and the horses needed for ranching and transportation.

On the third day, we were treated to a beautiful sight: six Clydesdale horses kept, we later found out, as a hobby by the owner. They had their own private pasture well fenced not only to keep them in but to kept intruders out. I let the crew take a break to watch the magnificent animals, the oohs and ahs flowing freely, then back to work.

On the fourth day, while traversing the biggest pasture yet a humbling event took place. A rail fence had been installed somewhere in the middle of the pasture and we couldn't understand why—at first—as we ducked or climbed over the rails. And then, we found out why, a big red bull about four hundred feet away. He occupied himself servicing a half-dozen cows he claimed for himself. I thought, *Good. That'll keep him busy.*

Not having had any experience with any kind of bull, I asked old Joe if he thought the bull would stay where he is. That was a mistake.

"Ah, just let him come over here and I'll hit him right on the nose with my stick." Joe always carried a substantial walking stick with him, why I never knew because he didn't need it, being in great shape and quite agile on his feet. Having boasted what he would do, old Joe started mooing at the bull.

"Joe, what the fuck are you doing?" I asked alarmed. "He's minding his own business. Leave him alone."

But old Joe continued mooing even louder, apparently looking for a confrontation. With that, the bull looked up and stared intently at Joe—probably sizing up the rest of us as well. Joe still wouldn't stop antagonizing him. Suddenly, first one front hoof then the second front hoof started kicking dirt backwards.

"Joe, stop, God damn it!" But Joe kept on mooing the bull.

Too late, all four hoofs kicked dirt now. Finished warning us, he came on like a thunderous locomotive, head down, horns pointed in our direction, dirt and grass flying everywhere around him. I could feel the ground vibrate where I stood from the pounding of his hoofs under his two thousand pounds.

The men scrambled and so did I. In a wide-open area, we couldn't make it to the fence and there weren't many trees. We got in each other's way trying to climb the nearest one. Wouldn't you know it, old Joe was the first one up. And that's where we stayed, the bull underneath still snorting, eyeing us, and refusing to leave.

I was really angry. "Now look what the fuck you've done, Joe," I yelled at him as he sat on a branch in a nearby tree. "John isn't going to like this. No way. Next time you listen to me."

We hung, clung, and tried to ease our tiring muscles and aching butts as best we could for a couple of hours, our lunches lying scattered on the ground. The bull sniffed some of the bags, not interested, his only interest being us. Every now and then he pawed the ground to show he still meant business and grew more and more impatient with our not coming down. Everyone, shouting from tree to tree, cursed old Joe and even insulted him.

"What do you expect from an old fart?" yelled Luke.

Even mellow Jim chimed in. "I guess Joe's losing it, poor old man."

"What do you mean losing it?" questioned Eduardo. "He's already lost it."

And then old eagle-eyed Joe spoke up. "Wait a minute. I can see John coming."

We all looked in the direction Joe pointed, but no one saw what old Joe saw. "He may be a half mile away but he's coming," insisted old Joe.

"So what's he going to do?" asked Mike.

"And you can be the one to explain how the hell this happened, Joe," said Austin.

"And if you try to bullshit him, I'll tell him," added Luke.

"Now, just wait a minute, you guys, all of you," I said, having to shout them down. "I'm the boss, and I'll do the talking."

"But--" said Luke and Austin together.

"No buts. John looks to me to run things, and when they don't go as they should, it's me he's going to come down on as to why. So I'll do the talking."

"He the boss," said Jim. "And I see to it he is." Everyone quieted down. No one messed with Big Jim.

John had at last drawn close, perhaps a couple hundred feet. He eyed the bull—and the bull eyed him.

"My, my, what do we have here?" he said with a disapproving tone. His eyes shifted from tree to tree. "A bunch of candy asses."

With that, John pulled an ordinary white hanker chef from his back pocket. He let it hang by holding one corner and while waving it gently from left to right, took a few steps toward the bull. The red bull, reluctant to leave his quarry, eyed him menacingly. Still, John advanced and kept gently waving his hanker chef. The bull pawed the ground. John drew closer and closer to him, the bull's eyes seemingly more fixed on the hanker chef than John. At about fifty feet the bull bucked his head and snorted what could have been a final warning: don't come any closer. But John did. They were now, at the most, a possible twenty feet apart. At this point, John took only baby steps, but still moved closer and closer.

I couldn't believe what I was seeing. Utter silence reigned, everyone mesmerized. "That guy's got guts," someone murmured.

John and the bull were no more than ten feet apart now, their eyes locked, John's steps only inches, and always the very gentle waving of the hanker chef. Suddenly, the bull backed up a step. John advanced. Again, the bull backed up a step or two. Again, John advanced, John's challenge without attacking evidently too much for the bull to understand. He didn't know what to make of it. The bull slowly turned and walked away back toward his harem.

"You bunch of pussies can all come down now and have your lunch."

Once the crew had scrambled, shimmied, and jumped down from their retreats, they gave John a big round of applause. Then they grabbed their brown bags, plopped down slumped up against a tree, and chowed down..

John made it clear he didn't need an explanation, saying he knew how temperamental bulls can be. "Some can be very territorial and come after you for no other reason at all."

In view of what John said, I saw no reason to explain. Something more important had to be addressed now. I initially wanted to give John two-week notice which had now dwindled to eleven days. I couldn't put it off any longer. I made up my mind I would do it that night when we got back in our room. John's restless nightmares would probably get worse.

We sat on our beds talking about the job, how much progress had been made, and our goal for the next three days. John seemed oblivious to what I had told him when he interviewed me. I had been right up front with him and told him I'd have to leave when I called my buddy to see when his furlough started so I could get to his base in time to take him home. Now, mid-May, that time had come. Without further hesitation I reminded John of that.

"Damn, I completely forgot about that," replied John. "I guess I assumed once you got into the job and all that good money you'd want to stay."

"I do like the job and the pay and the guys. It's given me tremendous experience that I never would have gotten back home."

"So why can't you let your buddy take a bus?"

"Because he doesn't have much money but mainly because I gave him my word. He's counting on me and I don't want to let him down."

John looked thoroughly deflated, like a balloon that had seen better days, his dejection pronounced. "What the fuck am I going to do."

"Can't you advertise again? There's got to be other surveyors around looking for work, maybe even older guys with way more surveying experience than me."

"You may be young, Don, and not all that experienced, but you've done one hell of a job. Even a licensed surveyor could not have done any better. And not all surveyors can handle a crew the way you do or be willing to work in the bayou for that matter."

"Well, thanks for all the compliments, John. You're making me feel guilty. You've been good to me and now I feel I'm leaving you in a jam."

"Well, you did tell me. I remember now. I'll just have to make some quick phone calls to get advertisements in a few papers tomorrow. Shit."

John pulled a pint whiskey flask that he always carried from his rear pocket and took a slug. One not being enough, he took another then, held it out to me. I didn't really feel like drinking, but I took it just to be sociable and empathetic. Before long, the flask was drained. He pulled a half-empty bottle from his beat-up suitcase.

"Gee, I'm sorry, John."

"Don't apologize. You got to do what you got to do."

We got drunk.

We pushed hard to get as much done as we could in the remaining eleven days. John succeeded in finding another surveyor unlicensed but a well experienced party chief of about thirty-five. He went out on the job with me. I introduced him to the crew and briefed him on how we handle laying out the pipeline route. He chuckled over my youth but voiced respect for what I had accomplished. He had no trouble taking over during the last two days.

That last day, after I had packed and gotten myself ready to leave in the morning, the men cornered me on the hotel porch. They had a going-away present for me. Big Jim acted as spokesperson.

"We want you to know we all think you were a great boss, in spite of being just a young whippersnapper." Everyone laughed. "We respect you. You're the first Yankee we've taken a liking to, and that's saying a lot—Yankee." Again, they all laughed.

"Give it to him," Mike said, apparently growing impatient.

"Yeah, give it to him, Jim," chimed in old Joe and the others.

"Okay. Here's something for you to wear wherever you go to keep God close."

"Wear?" I said, puzzled.

"Yes, wear. It'll keep you conscious that God is always with you, walking with you."

Jim handed me a small box not too well wrapped. I tore away the flimsy wrapping, opened the box, and inside saw what looked like a little jewelry box. I opened it and saw, resting on blue felt, a golden crucifix and chain, the crucifix staff about an inch and half long.

"Holy mackerel! It's beautiful. I don't know what to say."

"Will you wear it and never take it off?" Jim asked.

"Absolutely." I gingerly took it from the box and placed the necklace around my neck. The crucifix hung just right.

"But I thought you didn't believe in God," someone said.

"I never said that. Yes, I admit, I questioned whether God really existed. But I never said he didn't either. And after knowing you guys, I do believe there is a God now."

"That makes me very happy," said Jim.

"And just so you know," added Mike, "not only is the crucifix pure gold, so is the chain."

"Nothing but the best for God . . . and for you," added Jim.

. . .

It would be a long drive to Shreveport, over three hundred miles, so I wanted to get an early start. I got on the road before anyone else rose. One last look at tormented John all tangled up in his bedding, pillow on the floor, and I quietly left.

I headed east back toward Louisiana and crossed the state line around eleven o'clock. An occasional cotton farm bordered the road as I drove. I'd be looking for U.S. Highway 171 which went directly north to Shreveport. My stomach grumbled letting me know I hadn't eaten breakfast. I also needed to relieve myself. I stopped at a diner around two in the afternoon and had a sumptuous cheeseburger with mustard on one side and mayonnaise on the other, just like a lot of the natives. Then I got back on the road.

I don't know what made me think the old Plymouth could run forever on its own as I viewed the gauge on empty. I'd have to stop at a gas station and hit the John again while at it.

Night descended. Out in the sparsely populated boondocks with no street lights, the so-called highway became nothing more than a darkened two-lane country road. With its constant up and down and occasional sharp curves and the pitch blackness, I felt unnerved.

I had about a hundred miles to go when it started. A big trailer truck came up behind me so close its headlights in my rearview mirror practically blinded me. I floored the gas pedal and managed to pull away, but the driver refused to let me go. He quickly closed the gap and rode my ass again, and now started honking his horn. Again, I floored the pedal, but something was wrong. I knew the car could do ninety, but I couldn't get it to go over fifty. Sometimes going downhill, the Plymouth would reach sixty, but forty-five proved to be tops going uphill after another fifty miles or so. This enabled him to stay right on top of me.

I got scared. This guy, most likely a redneck, probably hated Yankees which, of course, he could see from my New Jersey plates. He could easily push me right off the road and, out in this forsaken country, no one would be the wiser.

He tailed me so close now I couldn't even see his headlights, all the while honking his extremely loud horn. No shoulder existed to either side, only ditches and woods and he knew it. Otherwise, I would have pulled over and let him pass. He had every intention of continuing to harass me—if not worse.

I thought, *well, maybe this is it for me.* I took a deep breath and admonished myself. *Pull yourself together, Don. You've just lived through alligators, water moccasins, and an angry red bull. You didn't go to pieces then, and now you're going to go to pieces? Remember what Jim said: God is always with you, walking with you.* I found that thought comforting and calming as I ran my fingers over the crucifix. *Well, if ever I needed your help, God, I need it now.*

My redneck friend continued to crowd me, and there was nothing I could do about it. Minutes later, I saw some light up ahead, perhaps coming from a little hamlet. I spotted a small gas station where the owner had left one light on over a Gulf sign. I turned sharply into the station skidding on the gravel. My nemesis zoomed by still honking his horn. I breathed easier. While sitting there, I caught my hands trembling. After a few minutes, I took another deep breath and got out on the road again.

It was four in the morning when I pulled into Shreveport. I still had to find the airbase, and I knew everyone would be sacked out yet for the most part. So I parked in a market parking lot and decided to sleep in the car for a few hours. I needed some shuteye badly.

I awoke to daylight at nine. I had really conked out. I felt reenergized and wasted no time asking an old man for directions to the base. Ten minutes later, I arrived and told the guard why. He picked up the intercom and got the word to Frank. A half-hour later, Frank came out all smiles and carrying his duffle bag.

"Hey, man, I see you made it," he said as we hugged.

"I said I would, didn't I, you bum. Throw your duffle bag in the back. Let's get going." We couldn't stop talking all the way home, him about the air force, me about alligators, water moccasins, and red bulls.

Soon the Plymouth wouldn't go over thirty-five. Before it quit altogether, we stopped at a gas station in Baltimore that advertised a repair shop. But no repairs were needed. The sharp mechanic found the problem in a few minutes. The cover on the carburetor had a felt lining and, from old age, the felt had disintegrated and got sucked into the carburetor instead of just air. He said the felt is supposed to filter the air before it mixes with the gas. "Remove the felt altogether from the underside of the cover and drive without it. Get a new cover when you get home." He didn't want any money, but I slipped him a five anyway. Mystery solved.

I dropped Frank off at his house and headed for that rundown tenement I called home. Frank and I had already decided to go out that same night and make up for lost time. There were so many friends and girls to hook up with again at our favorite hangout, Nick's Grove.

Yes, I was back, but I wasn't the same guy who had left just three short months before. I sensed I had grown from a teenager searching for his true self to a young man now more confident of his manhood, my father's disdain notwithstanding. I had arrived. Nothing would ever be the same.

EPILOGUE

Careful Where You Step

We've all heard the saying: "We all travel the same road," meaning we're all human and experience the same trials and tribulations in life. But after having written *"Careful Where You Step"*, in reflection, all of us do not necessarily travel the same road; do we? For some of us, that road can be quite different and difficult to navigate.

"Careful Where You Step" is a memoir of a troubled youth, a young man—me—having his doubts about just how much of a man he really is. Doubt instilled by an unapproving father who held him at arms-length. Don's true and challenging adventure in Louisiana and Texas is told here exactly as it happened.

But beyond the alligators and tornados of Louisiana and the red bulls of Texas lies the deeper story, the heart of the story. The story of a youth, never accepted by his rough and tough, hard-drinking father as measuring up to the kind of son he envisioned having. How could that youth not feel his father's disdain and lack of respect or love for him? Is it any wonder that Don felt this terrible need to prove himself, not just to his father but to himself. Does he succeed? Having read his story, you decide.

Many years have passed since, though wet behind the ears, I ventured into the realm of manhood. But the whole experience is still so vivid in my memory that it seems like I lived it only yesterday. I didn't fully realize it at the time but, looking back, in just three short months, those events changed me from being an insecure youth to a more confident young man in the true sense of the word. In short, those three months had a profound life-changing impact on my life, not only back then but on who I am today. I guess it always will.

As to that other crucial issue concerning God: I'm still not a church-goer, but I do believe in God . . . more than ever. I speak to Him every day, and He speaks to me. And I'm still wearing the crucifix Jim, Mike, and the crew gave me when we gathered on that hotel porch in Texas many years ago to say our goodbyes. They taught me the true meaning of camaraderie, friendship, and love, which helped end my running feud with a God I supposedly *didn't* believe in. I'll never forget them. And yes, I got my old job back and went on to become a Professional Land Surveyor.

. . .

I tell this story because it led to my writing *"Does God Exist?"* many years later. Were it not for what happened in *"Careful Where You Step"*, most likely I would have never written *"Does God Exist?"*, for can you imagine it being written by an atheist?

I was changed by Jim and Mike and never would be the same. With no exaggeration, I found myself in a dazed-like state of mind even long after returning home, overwhelmed with the sudden enlightenment that had engulfed me. I felt compelled to share that enlightenment with others that are less fortunate, but how? Many years passed before I finally decided to do just that—by writing a book. I spent six years researching proof of God's existence, now strengthened by many *new discoveries*. From that research emerged *"Does God Exist?"* Here it is.

DOES GOD EXIST?
New Discoveries
Are Science and the Belief in God Compatible?

Is there a God, a Universal Power, a Supreme Being? That's the eternal question that has weighed heavily on the heart of humanity since time immemorial. A definitive answer, proof as skeptics and outright non-believers demand, still eludes us. That much of one's belief in God revolves around faith goes without saying. But when I gaze up at the awe-inspiring universe or behold nature in all its grandeur here on Earth, for me, the answer comes: God exists! I admit I can't prove this, but neither can non-believers prove God does not exist, Darwinism notwithstanding, as we shall see.

There are many questions to which we just don't have the answers, says Neil de Grasse Tyson, an astrophysicist, and James Trefil, physicist, in their ground-breaking book, *Cosmic Queries*. And until we do have the answers, we cannot dismiss the possible existence of an all-powerful God. For instance: What is the origin of life? The unproven theory that life spontaneously sprang from nonliving matter has been debunked. And the idea that all cells come from other cells, while seemingly true, raises another question: Where did the first cell come from? Questions like these are simply ignored by scientists since, on one hand, they simply don't know, but on the other hand, they aren't about to admit that maybe God had something to do with it.

There is an inconvenient truth evolutionists can't explain and don't want to deal with. They would have you believe they've proven evolution occurs from one genus (family of animal life) to another genus based upon, for instance, the variations induced by scientists' *deliberately controlled breeding* of the fruit fly which, because it has a very short lifespan, lends itself to breeding many generations in a very short time. But after decades of trying, no matter what variations come from this *controlled breeding,* scientists have found a fruit fly is still a fruit fly (the same species they started with), not a new genus, i.e., a new family of animal life.

Scientists may also have to go back to the drawing board when it comes to Dark Matter and Dark Energy, which comprise ninety-five percent of the universe. In his book, Tyson says: 'We know it exists; we have no idea what it is; perhaps it should instead be called "dark gravity."' This kind of dovetails with an article that appeared in The Press of Atlantic City April 8, 2021, entitled, "Results of two experiments defy physics rulebook."

The experiments challenge how physicists say the universe works on a subatomic level. All matter, including space, are comprised of particles. But particles like the muon may not be living in the seemingly empty spaces between the other particles as thought. There's something that "seems to fill in all the space and time." Physicist David Kaplan of John Hopkins University says, "That something could be explained by a new particle or force" [Not yet discovered.] May I suggest that perhaps our concept of God may not be quite accurate? Could that force be God himself holding the whole universe that he created, not the Big Bang, together? Could it be the "God Particle" that some talk about that fills in all that space and time?

As brilliant as scientists are, they aren't always right. For decades physicists believed the expansion of the universe, the result of the purported Big Bang explosion, was slowing down as the force of the initial explosion dissipated. Then, along come physicists Riess, Perlmutter, and Schmidt, who proved just the opposite: the universe's expansion is accelerating. Even Einstein's 1905 General Theory of Relativity, which says nothing is faster than the speed of light, upending Sir Isaac Newton's long-held theory on gravity, is threatened. Scientists at CERN, the world's largest accelerator and physics lab, also recently shocked the scientific world, saying they've clocked neutrinos traveling faster than light. Both of these revelations shake the very foundation of many laws accepted for centuries in physics, astronomy, and cosmology. But those laws were promulgated by scientists, not nature. Are they valid? Let's ponder what was believed and accepted centuries ago.

> "The Laws of Nature dictated by God himself is Superior to any other. It is binding over all the Globe, in all Countries, and at all times. No human laws are of any validity if contrary to this," ...

Here we have a basic—yet profound—observation made over 200 hundred years ago by the renowned English jurist, Sir William Blackstone (1723 – 1780). Blackstone's perception of the Laws of Nature relative to life on earth is as true and relevant to our existence today as it was back then. There are natural laws that govern the workings of our entire cosmos, our galaxy, our solar system, right down to our planet. These universal laws were around long before humanity and are very precise and ingenious laws that automatically maintain continuity. *Today's scientists cannot change them just to put those laws in sync with their beliefs.*

That some of our more open-minded and honest scientists are now conceding there's at least the possibility of a God points to a significant break in the solidarity exacted by the scientific community concerning this contentious issue, under the threat of otherwise being ostracized. We are now witness to this split within the ranks of scientists as exemplified by leading astronomers such as Robert Jastrow, who is credited with this observation: Now we see how the astronomical evidence leads to a biblical view of the origin of the world. The details differ, but the essential elements in the astronomical and biblical accounts of Genesis are the same.

During the 19th century, when the many fossil discoveries seemed to undermine Creation according to the Book of Genesis, William Buckland, the British prime minister, theologian, geologist, and paleontologist, upended geologists turning their own findings against them. He asked: How come the author of Genesis [meaning God] knew the order of origins: first water populations, second air populations, then land populations, and humans last of all? Obviously, only the Creator could have had that knowledge way back then, while we from fossil records are only finding this out in the 19th century.

Though considered blasphemous in the scientific community, many scientists are rethinking this idea of Intelligent Design. In an interview by David Ewing Duncan for Discovery Magazine, Francis Collins, one of the world's foremost scientists and former head of the Hunan Genome Project —the cataloging of all human chromosomes and the genes each one contains—and author of The Language of God: A Scientist's Evidence for Belief who says to hard-core, atheistic scientists like Richard Dawkins: Is there any dogma more unsupported by the facts than from the scientist who stands up and says, 'I know there is no God'? Collins adds: The God of the Bible is also the God of the gnome. Here we see the compatibility of religion and science emerging.

Scientists aren't the only ones doing an about-face and finding God. Author Dan Brown, who wrote "The Da Vinci Code," made a study of the Bible and decided it didn't make sense while science did, causing him to pull away from religion. He now says he's come full circle as a result of studying science, and the further one delves into science, the mushier the ground gets. You start to see there is an order and spiritual aspect to science. This, again, suggests that science and religion are compatible.

We have the hypothesis, and that's all it is, a theory, that the entire universe was born of the so-called Big Bang, vast matter so densely compacted in on itself to the size of a marble by gravity that it became intensely heated, exploded and, bingo, the universe. But this theory too leads to more questions: Where did that matter come from? And what came before the Big Bang?

Scientists accept the Big Bang Theory in spite of admitting there's a 500-million- year blank they refer to as the "Dark Ages" in which they cannot explain how we went from a gas-filled universe to one filled with galaxies and what we see in the night sky today. But so what? We scientists say the Big Bang occurred and that's all that's to it.

To go further, a recent discovery, in my opinion, shows that, once again, our scientists have stumbled with their long-accepted Big Bang Theory. All explosions gradually dissipate once they've reached their maximum outer limits from the force, then collapse and fall back in on themselves. That's not what's happening with our universe, as recently discovered. Not only is our universe continuing to expand, its rate of expansion is actually accelerating, as discovered by physicists and stated before, not slowing down in direct contradiction of how all explosions work, refuting the Big Bang Theory. How do our scientists explain this? They don't. They simply ignore whatever doesn't fit their ideology or, perhaps more accurately, their agenda: There is no God.

Let's think about the birth of the universe for a moment. No matter how far back in time we go, including the questionable super-dense, pea-sized matter from which the "Big Bang" supposedly exploded, we are always left with that nagging question: Now where did that pea-sized matter come from? Astrophysicist Saul Perlmutter of the University of California at Berkeley admits we don't know what existed or happened before that. But it seems other scientists are working hard to invent ways of figuring out what happened just before that moment. And to say the universe always existed or nothing at all existed prior to the universe—as some scientists are now resorting to in order to get around this inconvenient question—doesn't make total sense. The metaphysical premise that says: "from nothing only nothing comes" renders such a position absurd, thus pointing the way to the likelihood of a transcendent cause. Or put another way, to say the universe came into being on its own somehow while nothing existed before it is mind-boggling. How could the universe create itself if it didn't exist to begin with? Again, we're back to the only sensible explanation: it didn't create itself. God did. For anything made of matter and energy had to have a beginning, had to come into existence at some point and time. How? When? It is only an all-powerful, Supreme Being who would not need to have had a beginning simply because ... He is God!

But scientists don't give in too easily, even when they don't know the answer to the above nagging question. The newer Big Bang Model argues that time is only a physical feature of the universe and only came into existence because of the Big Bang. Therefore, scientists say it is illogical to ask what came before. What a convenient and totally unproven theory to get around the question of where the universe came from and what existed before it. Forgive me, but my take on this unproven theory concerning time is that it's just a copout for a question they can't answer. When trapped, come up with another theory and demand that it be accepted simply because scientists say so.

Let's move on and touch upon the Bible a little. In Genesis 1: 1-2, it is first stated, "The earth was without form and void ..." This implies the Earth already existed prior to the seven days of creation which, if true, would remove any contradiction between the Bible and how old scientists say the Earth is. It could be any age. Also, the seventh day, when God rested, can be shown to be an epoch day, not a 24-hour day, and to be 7000 years long based upon Bible chronology. That day is not yet over, according to theologians. Again, if all this is true, logic dictates that each of the preceding six days of creation were epoch days also and not the 24-hour day as we know it.

Stay with creation for a moment. Three evolutionary biologists (not theologians): Gilbert of Harvard, Dorst of Yale, and Akashi of the University of Chicago, as a result of their genetic research, concluded that man's forefather was a single individual. Could this be Adam? Later, American molecular biologist, Michael Hammer, came to the same conclusion. And yet again, a group of British geneticists agreed that all humans descended from one man. In 1987, a study of mitochondrial DNA (all cells contain mitochondria, the furnace that produces our heat and energy) which is only passed on from mother to daughter, proved all females descended from one woman. Could this be Eve? I'm just asking. You decide.

Many argue that if God does exist, why doesn't he give us some sort of sign to prove it? Something we can hang our beliefs on. Well, maybe God did. Maybe there have been signs right under our collective noses all the while, but we fail to attach the significance to them they deserve, like the Shroud of Turin. Tiny pieces have been allowed to be cut from it for study and testing but all attempts to prove The Shroud is not old enough and that the image thereon is not that of Jesus have failed. And then we have the Dead Sea Scrolls written on papyrus and parchment used in Jesus's time. They were found in 1947 in a cave near the ancient Jewish settlement of Qumran in the hills of the Judean desert and likely hidden around A.D. 70. They are the oldest biblical texts ever found. There are sufficient fragments to confirm the age and authenticity of today's Bible, including a fragment containing the first few lines of the Book of Genesis, describing the creation of the world. Other scrolls have been found since, lending further credence to the Shroud's and the Bible's authenticity.

But for the skeptics, here's something more tangible we're all more familiar with, the *perfect* symmetry of a total solar eclipse. Our sun is 400 times larger than our moon, but it is also 400 times farther from us, producing the *perfect* mathematical ratio necessary to create the optical illusion of the sun and the moon appearing to be the same size and, thus, making it possible for a *perfect* solar eclipse. Coincidence or deliberate? Mathematicians say the odds of this happening randomly are monumental, leading them and more scientists to say it could only be that our solar system was *fine-tuned*. Is it any wonder that so many prominent cosmologists, physicists, and mathematicians have come to embrace the Anthropic Principle, in essence, that the universe and our solar system were given such properties (read Intelligent Design) so as to make our Earth suitable for intelligent life.

Thomas Jefferson, a student of natural history, believed that life on Earth could not have risen by chance but only by Intelligent Design. That was quite an advanced forward-looking position to take back then and contrary to what was to come later, Darwin's theory of evolution by natural selection, which the growing secular world, being atheistic, came to unabashedly insist was a proven fact which, of course, it was not.

Let me digress once again and talk about purpose; God's purpose.

For everything that exists, there is a purpose for its being. Purpose is an integral part of Natural Law. Is this not a self-evident truth, for what other reason could there be for anything to come into existence but to serve a very specific purpose? Let's examine what I propose is intertwined with the very essence of life and is an undeniable reflection of Intelligent Design: purpose.

First came the universe to propagate stars, planets, gravity, light, including our own sun and solar system. Our sun's purpose: to hold Earth in place and provide it with light and heat for the benefit of life. And need we ask what the Earth's purpose is? Simply put, our Earth's purpose is to provide a livable habitat for all life, plant, and animal. And the Earth accomplishes this with its rotation and tilt on its axis so as to bring about the changes in season from spring to summer to fall to winter and then back to spring again for the creation of new life, once more. The Earth is self-balancing and changing the seasons helps the Earth keep all life in balance. For it is through nature that the living Earth keeps things that are necessary for life in balance, which it must if the Earth is to remain habitable for all life, including us human beings.

Here are more examples that point toward the possibility of fine-tuning, each of which could be taken as another sign of God's existence. A planet has to be in a "habitable zone" relative to its sun, and its orbit must be circular—not oval like most planets in other solar systems—so as to maintain relatively constant temperatures within reasonable ranges in order to be stable and support life. The Earth meets both of these requirements. By chance?

It's been said that the Earth is a living entity on its own. Seismologists agree the Earth pulsates every 26 seconds but don't know why. They've even located the origin, a single source in the

Gulf of Guinea along the western coast of Africa, but still don't know why. The mysterious pulse has been tracked since the 1960s. And why is the pulsing so rhythmic? It could be of no great significance but, on the other hand, could beg the question: Does the Earth have a heart, so to speak, like all living things in keeping with the Earth being a living entity in its own?

The Earth is the only planet known to have *free-standing* water, which happens to cover three-quarters of its surface and, as we all know, is necessary for life of any kind. If we were slightly closer to the sun, the oceans would boil and evaporate. If we were slightly farther, they would freeze. Was this just pure luck or another sign of . . . Intelligent Design?

The Earth is marvelously *self-balancing* in many ways. For instance: animal life produces carbon dioxide necessary for and absorbed by plant life; plant life produces oxygen and food necessary for animal life. Plants also make their own self-sustaining food through photosynthesis, another miraculous process in itself.

The Earth's gravitational field is strong enough to protect us from the sun's gamma rays while still letting through enough of the sun's heat and light necessary for both plant and animal life, another carefully balanced (fine-tuned) interaction between the Earth and sun.

Another possible example of a sign coming from a Supreme Being to show that he exists could be his fine-tuning of a certain flower that looks like a particular female bee. As such, it attracts and entices the male to make love to it and, in so doing, pollinate it. This is not something to be taken with a yawn. This is astounding! Does anyone really believe that this just came about randomly somehow? Which, for me, would be a little too far-fetched to accept. But then, if not randomly, how did the flower come to know to do this? Are we to assume the flower has a brain of sorts or at least enough reasoning power to say to itself: "I'm going to make myself look like that female bee so the male will copulate with me, sneaky little devil that I am." Which is even more far-fetched. No. I submit that it is just another sign of God's handiwork, of his existence.

How about one last sign of fine-tuning by God? this one affecting human beings directly. In humans, the voice box is positioned lower in the throat than in any other primate, equipping us with a one-of-a-kind resonating system. This unique attribute is stunning in that it enables a wide range of sounds absolutely necessary in order for us to speak—and sing—so extensively, unheard of in the animal world. Did God design this exception in us because he wanted to make us the exception to all other life? Could this be another sign of his deliberate handiwork?

As we progress, notice how all life is intertwined, is interdependent. No life lives in a vacuum. This obvious truth is reflected in an old Native American belief:

The Earth does not belong to man. Man belongs to the Earth.

All things are connected like the blood that unites a family.

Man does not weave the web of life, he is only a strand in it.

Fred Hoyle, a former avowed atheist and the dean of cosmology, who authored the theory of the "Static Universe" which eliminated the need for a Creator or God has, like an increasing number of scientists, also done an about-face and has even attacked some of Richard Dawkins' theories, blasphemy in the scientific community for sure. Hoyle came to the conclusion that without a super-intellect—read Intelligent Design—life on Earth could not exist. Perhaps what Hoyle was driving at is that the Earth is intrinsically bound to the universe, and, by following universal laws—God's laws—is incredibly self-balancing, as stated before, making life on

Earth possible. Thus, by extension, isn't it possible that the entire universe has also been deliberately fine-tuned the same as our Earth and solar system?

In the face of all this latest research and contradictory arguments, some evolutionists are now back to clinging to the old idea of a "prebiotic soup" that purportedly contained all the necessary elements for the spontaneous formation of life. Here again, Hoyle steps in with a powerful rebut. He equates the probability of such an event occurring to the chance that a tornado sweeping through a junkyard might assemble a Boeing 747 from the material therein. Ridiculous and impossible, wouldn't you say?

Even Anthony Flew, Dawkins' fellow professor at Oxford and considered among the world's most important philosophers, for many years opposed the idea there was a Supreme Being, yet changed his mind in 2004 and embraced God, saying: The argument to Intelligent Design is enormously stronger than when I first met it. He went further: It now seems to me that the findings of more than fifty years of DNA research have provided materials for a new and enormously powerful argument to design.

All this does not matter to atheists and die-hard scientists who refuse to even acknowledge, let alone accept new and tangible discoveries made by archeologists. They continue their push to discredit the Bible, including that Jesus was not the Son of God and may not have even existed. How can they be so inflexible in view of the many recent new archeological discoveries such as:

Stone vessels were highly valued for purification rituals in preference to clay or glass. The stone vessels were a daily part of the lives of the Jewish population back in the first century. Jesus used one at a wedding in Cana in which he turned water to wine, his first miracle, which is, of course, pooh-poohed by non-believers. But the Gospel of John 2:6 relates that there was a workshop for crafting stone vessels in Galilee in northern Israel. Archeologists have long searched for such a stone workshop and, led by archeologist Yonatan Adler of Ariel University, found a first-century stone vessel factory near the ancient settlement of Cana not far from where the wedding took place. This substantiates the Gospel by John and his depiction of the wedding and miracle performed by Jesus using one of those stone vessels that is said to have taken place near Cana.

Let's take a look at one more recent discovery. Found the remnants of the hull of a boat exposed, lying in the mud of the Sea of Galilee due to a severe drought. The boat was long enough to accommodate at least thirteen people, which would dovetail nicely with Jesus and his twelve disciples when it is said they sailed the Galilee. Carbon 14 testing confirmed its age as dating back to the time of Jesus. How about that? Once again, what is written in the Bible is substantiated.

Those that believe in Darwin's Theory of Evolution as an alternative to creationism seem more certain of Darwinism than Darwin himself. He admits in *The Origin of Species,* that failure to find any fossils of any species in the in-between transitional stage (absolutely necessary to validate his theory) "perhaps, is the most obvious and gravest objection which can be urged against my theory." And I think it's important here to emphasize what Darwin admits: his theory is just that only a theory, not proof of evolution.

This leads me to ask why so many prominent scientists throughout the world are beginning to now see what they didn't or refused to see before? Were they non-believers mainly because, as scientists, they had to be atheists; they had to insist on incontrovertible proof of God's existence? Or were they atheists because they couldn't accept that a good God would allow so many bad things to happen and, therefore, couldn't exist? But if we're looking for reasons why bad things happen, let's not overlook that within Darwin's Theory of Evolution reside two tenets coined by Herbert Spencer: the "struggle for existence" and "survival of the fittest." The roots of Nazism have their source in the writings of Friedrich Nietzsche whose philosophy of the superhuman drew from those writings of Darwin and Spencer.

Perhaps scientists, like so many others, became atheists because atrocities, such as the Crusades and the Inquisition, were fueled by religion, as is much of today's terrorism. But *people* are behind all religions, and *they*, not God, will use religion as a subterfuge to further their own selfish agenda and do bad things. (A gun can do no harm without someone behind it pulling the trigger.) On the contrary, I contend that bad things are more likely to happen in the absence of God, not because of Him. Or to enlarge upon what Albert Einstein said when he was still a student: Just as cold is the absence of heat, and darkness is the absence of light … I believe evil is the absence of good or, more pointedly, God.

But I'm not going to sidestep the aforementioned argument made by atheists and, in all fairness, is pondered even by many of those who do believe in God. Okay, they say, so it's people who do all these bad things, but still, God doesn't have to allow it to happen. True. But if God controlled our every thought and action instead of granting us free will, we would be reduced to nothing but robots. No one would be able to think for himself or live the life he chose to live. God would be living our lives for us. There would be no individualism. We would be emotionally and psychologically enslaved. What kind of a life would that be?

No. We were given free will so we could each live our own life. And, perhaps, so God could see what we do with that life. For does it not follow that if we were denied free will by God so as make us unable to do bad, then, likewise, we would also be unable to *voluntarily* do good.

How about natural calamities? I told you right up front, I too don't have all the answers. But, for what it's worth, let me contemplate the possibilities from a religious perspective. Perhaps calamities happen to test our faith. Perhaps since Adam and Eve and all the people that followed sinned and, thus, were no longer perfect, God felt man had not earned and did not deserve a perfect world either, i.e., paradise. Perhaps that will come later, but right now, we have volcanoes, tornadoes, and earthquakes as part of our punishment. We bring some of it upon ourselves, like building in a river plain that's known to flood, or at the bottom slopes of a volcano, or practically on top of the ocean. And some of these calamities we actually help bring about. For instance, a monstrous El Nino would not develop without the massive hole in the ozone layer we've heard so much about. And how did that hole get there? From pollution created by man, rooted in his greed and selfishness in pursuit of materialism and profit, i.e., never being satisfied. We have to learn the hard way, like the child that burns its finger on a hot stove. And perhaps when humanity stops being so greedy, selfish, and destructive, the punishments—natural disasters—will also stop. That makes at least a little sense. But, admittedly, it is a difficult question to which only God, if he exists, knows the answer.

Let's stop a moment and think about some of the events prophesied in the Bible, the materialism mentioned above, for instance. Can anyone deny that societies the world over have become more materialistic? And at what cost? Faith. Faith in the Bible. Faith in the existence of God. In place of love of God, people love themselves *(2 Timothy 3:1-5)*. People want what they want materially regardless of the right or wrong of it. This attitude harbored by today's adults seeps down to their children and shows today in their lack of respect for their parents. Materialism fostered all this.

Here's another possible answer to why God allows evil in this world. We spoke before that God wanted us to have free will to see what we'd do with it, i.e., use it for good or for bad. Perhaps God also permits evil to prove that humanity without God will only result in man's inhumanity to man. After all, in the minds of many, if there is no God, then there is no right and wrong, so why be good.

The debate over creation and the existence of God has intensified, and now, even Darwinism is being challenged. Public Broadcasting System (PBS), in their 2001 television series, "Evolution," boldly asserted that all scientific evidence supports evolution, and virtually every reputable scientist in the world supports Darwin's Theory of Evolution. This is patently not true as proven by more recent evidence discovered and the declarations of a number of prominent scientists, some noted herein.

In 2008, The Vatican publicly admitted the possibility of aliens having visited Earth, meaning there could be life on other planets. Does this preclude the existence of God? No, says the Vatican, and this author agrees. For God could have created life throughout the universe, just as he could have used the Big Bang, if it actually happened, as a means to create the universe itself. Again, once we remove the dogmatism on both sides, we witness the emergence of religion and science becoming more compatible. Even Erich von Daniken, author of *Chariots of the Gods* and who believes Earth has been visited by aliens from outer space, nevertheless says he "believes in God and prays every night." To me, this suggests he must believe God created not only the Earth but the whole universe and any other inhabitants.

Repeated attempts by evolutionists to prove the transition from fish to amphibians to reptiles to birds and mammals (remember the fruit fly) had all failed when fossils showed that many supposed descendants were found to have lived before those from which they reputedly descended. No fossils of any species have been found in the in between transitional stage, i.e., partially developed changes, despite desperate claims to the contrary by scientists. Why not? With the tens of thousands of fossils discovered, they should abound. But they don't. This is true of the theoretical gradual transition of monkeys to apes to humans too. Don't believe everything you see on television. There has been a concerted effort by the non-believers to get the public to accept something that just has not been proven to be true. But again, for the sake of discussion, suppose evolution, as proffered by scientists, is true? This too God could have chosen to use as a means for the development of all life on Earth. Yes? No?

Some Darwinists and fossil enthusiasts got desperate to prove gradual transition had occurred.. In 1912, Charles Dawson and Arthur Smith Woodward, geologist at British Natural History Museum deliberately falsely claimed finding the missing link connecting ape to human, unearthing humanlike skull fragments and apelike jawbone from a gravel pit near Piltdown, England. They stained the bones to look older and filed down teeth from an orangutan so it would appear human. Atheistic extremists wouldn't you say? Fortunately, their hoax was exposed.

In the article, Origin Story – Our New Past, by Gemma Tarlsch, senior editor, in the April 2016 issue of Discover Magazine, it is shown just how uncertain we are as to the evolution of Homo sapiens. It is now being hotly debated whether it was Africa or Eurasia [from which we supposedly came]. Why? Because neither fossil nor genomic evidence supports either model.

Part of Darwin's Theory of Evolution is the tenet called gradualism, the slow process of evolutionary change. This gradualism has been challenged by a number of experts in the new field of "epigenetics": how the external environment can alter our genes and pass them on to future generations, a process much more rapid than Darwin's gradualism. We find that genetic mixing (grizzly bear/polar bear for instance) producing hybrids can happen very quickly due to rapid climate change in decades or just years, not centuries, according to Katherine Bagley, reporter for *Inside Climate News*. While there are many examples, a few will do.

Chicago University economist, Robert Fogel, says that over the past 300 years, humans have increased their average body size by over 50 percent, their average longevity by more than 100 percent. And, contrary to Darwin's gradual evolution, 300 years is the blink of an eye, a sneeze in the history of life.

Features that females prefer in order to choose their mates evolve very rapidly, says Yale University evolutionary ornithologist, Richard Prum. And, with that, another long-time accepted evolutionary theory is shot down, when Prum says feathers did not evolve from elongated scales; they are inborn.

Let's take one of my own first-hand experiences as a young man. When I worked as a land surveyor laying out the route for a new pipeline in the bayous of Louisiana, I saw cattle that had escaped from various farms and were living wild in the swamps. With their weight, I couldn't understand how they could get around in the muck without getting stuck. The men I was working with, who lived half the time in the bayous hunting alligators for shoes and pocketbooks, gave me a clue, which I eventually observed for myself. The cattle had quickly developed flayed hooves to better distribute their weight and help them get around. The time it took them to adapt isn't even a measurable fraction of a second in terms of the life of the universe or of evolution as Darwin proposes.

May I suggest from the above examples that the claim evolutionary changes take millions or even thousands or even hundreds of years to develop is not true. And if not true, how should this seeming contradiction to Darwin's Theory of Evolution affect our thinking as to how all present-day life came about?

Darwin's theory of evolution lacks *empirical evidence* as demanded by the scientific community for all other hypotheses. Why is the scientific community giving Darwin a free pass on this? In effect, *a priori:* deductive reasoning based upon theory instead of experience or experiment. Could it be that Darwinism is *their religion,* and, therefore, that's the way it has to be? During the "Cambrian Explosion," species displayed no gradual change but, on the contrary, just suddenly popped into existence without even the slightest indication of evolutionary ancestors as required by Darwin's theory. It's worth repeating that even Darwin lamented this lack of fossil evidence proving gradual change from genus to genus, prompting him to admit it was "the most obvious and gravest objection which can be urged against my theory."

In 1996, biochemist, Michael Behe, rocked the evolutionists' world with the publication of his book: *Darwin's Black Box: The Biochemical Challenge to Evolution.* Based upon what Behe called "irreducible complexity," he observed the thundering silence by scientists to publish any explanation of a Darwinian step-by-step origin of any complex biochemical system. It was his opinion that a science that fails to publish should perish.

Let's move on with some of my own observations. Selfless altruism is another thorn in the side of evolutionists, for it flies in the face of the offshoot of Darwinism expressed in the doctrine known as "Survival of the Fittest." In the battle for survival, evolutionists insist nothing can afford to be altruistic. That makes sense. And yet, we know altruism does exist in humanity—think, Mother Teresa—and, as suggested by the latest research, may even exist to a small degree among some of the higher animals.

I have long suspected many atheists *do* harbor an inherent but suppressed belief in God. When confronted with a threatening crisis, many may turn to God the same way believers do. This could be particularly true when faced with the possible loss of a loved one or when near death. When all else fails, this suppressed belief may very well surface and take charge, and, suddenly, the non-believer is a believer: *Oh, God, take me, not my child! Please, God, I don't want to die! God help me!*

An argument that could be made in support of God's existence is how he made us unique with special attributes, such as awareness not only of our surroundings but of ourselves, leading to our ability to ponder the future. Other creatures only concentrate on and take care of their more immediate needs by what's been conveniently dubbed instinct. But does this thing called instinct mean they have been preprogrammed, so to speak? In other words, if this seeming knowledge is inherent, built-in, and other animals are born with it, *how did that happen?* Or is this another indication of Intelligent Design we've heard so much about as some suggest? We don't need instinct, for we have the ability to project ourselves into the future: *What will I be when I grow up?* And later in life: *How shall I plan for my retirement?* As far as we know, no other creature thinks this way or is capable of mentally transporting itself to a time that still doesn't exist.

It is also generally accepted that other creatures lack a conscience. They do not debate if it's all right to steal the other guy's food or mate but are essentially guided instinctively to just take care of themselves. But we are not other creatures, are we? We hear that little voice inside called conscience that speaks to us. And no matter how hard we may try to ignore it—especially if it's expedient to do so—it constantly reminds us of the right and wrong of things, this Moral Law, which is another strong indication of his existence, a Supreme Being's presence. From conscience flows all those attributes people long to see in each other, attributes like fairness, sympathy, love. And I believe they flow from God to our conscience … if we're willing to listen. I ask: Are we certain conscience isn't God speaking to us?

Though a little technical, in her fine article, Seven Deadly Sins, Discover Magazine, September 2009, Kathleen McGowan perhaps puts us on the trail of where conscience may reside in the brain. According to Mario Beauregard of the University of Montreal, the right superior frontal gyrus and right anterior cingulated gyrus may regulate our impulses. These brain areas form a conscious self-regulating system, providing us with the evolutionarily unprecedented ability to control our own neural processing ... a feat achieved by no other creature. I'd like to suggest again that here too, we see the hand of the Creator in instilling us with a conscience, something no other creature has.

David P. Barash, evolutionary biologist at the University of Washington, admits there is plenty we don't know about the things we think we understand. One of the things he wonders about is why does separate sexuality (men and women) occur at all, when asexuality (both sexes contained in one creature) is so much more efficient and sure in propagating the species? May I be so bold as to step in here and suggest that that would be such a mundane experience for us as opposed to the terrible excitement and pleasure generated by the coupling of a man and woman, magnified immensely by the love they feel for each other.

While other higher animals are attached to and will defend their young, our emotions go well beyond that. There is this thing called love. This need we all have to love and be loved, a union of spirits, a blending of souls, another profound gift from God. How else can it be explained?

Without question, this need is intrinsic to our nature, our very essence. How do we explain this fundamental quality unique to humans? Could it be proof that God dwells within each of us? Since "God is love" (1 John 4:8), this inherent need to love and be loved could simply be another manifestation of a Supreme Being's presence. Listen to Ralph Waldo Emerson in his *Essay on Nature*:

"The current of the Universal Being circulates through me. I am part or particle of God."

With all this "scientific evidence" that purportedly proves there is no God—so-called proof that even many scientists no longer accept—let's not lose sight of the fact that if God does exist, and I believe there is ample reason to believe he does, God puts all our scientists to shame. For He is the greatest scientist of all. I further believe that, just as we plant the seed of the lovely lily in the rich earth to grow, so God plants the seed of his Spirit in each of us to grow. It's called the soul. And just as the seed of the lily seeks nourishment to flourish, so does our soul. The nourishment our soul seeks—and needs—is goodness, if it is to achieve birth and full fruition in the afterlife.

So I'm just going to keep living my life the way I believe God—and nature—intended. In my mind, they are one and the same, and since I feel one with nature, I guess that makes me one with God and that I always will be. This is the essence of me, Don Ackermann.

Who knows what awaits us on the other side? I don't. Scientists don't. Do you?

"The fool hath said in his heart, '*There is* no God.'" Psalm 14:1

Sources:

THE LANGUAGE OF GOD by Francis S. Collins

NEW PROOFS FOR THE EXISTENCE OF GOD by Robert J. Spitzer

DISCOVER Magazine

The Bible for Our Times, April 2007, and Creation Triumphs Over Evolution by Bible Students Congregation of New Brunswick [NJ].

THE HOLY BIBLE, Revised Standard Version

Cosmic Queries by Neil de Grasse Tyson and James Trefil

www.ingramcontent.com/pod-product-compliance
Lightning Source LLC
LaVergne TN
LVHW040200080526
838202LV00042B/3243